# INSIDE/OUT

Sibling Rivalry Press, LLC
PO Box 26147
Little Rock, AR 72221

info@siblingrivalrypress.com

www.siblingrivalrypress.com

ISBN: 978-1-943977-44-4

Library of Congress Control No. 2017957094

This title is housed permanently in the Rare Books and Special
Collections Vault of the Library of Congress.

First Sibling Rivalry Press Edition, January 2018

Aaron.
Baby, what can
I say to you.
I love you. respect you.
am grateful for your
work.

# INSIDE/OUT

Joseph Osmundson

Fuck fuck bsir! d::
but it's so hard:
let's keep an open
heart. All my love,
Always.

Sibling Rivalry Press
Little Rock, Arkansas
DISTURB/ENRAPTURE

Upside down
Boy, you turn me
Inside out
And round and round

— Diana Ross

# 1

Growing up, I was always outside. For my first three years of life, my family lived in the country, a mile from any roads. My mother figured that my sister and I running around naked would save her washing our cloth diapers. We were always outside and covered in dirt, forced to take a bath before dinner.

Or, maybe I should start with a story. It's about a different boy, one I can name. I grew up outside: Straight boys never made sense to me. I thought I was straight then, but by fifth grade, I knew my place. I was used to being with the girls or alone. In fifth grade, a boy—an easy, athletic, charming boy—seemed to want to be my friend. Chad. We had three of them in my class, but his last initial escapes me now. Maybe it was Chad R. He lived near my home and sat with me sometimes on the bus. He even called me at night, and so what if it was usually just to get help on his math homework.

But then it became only to get help on his math homework.

And he laughed along with the other kids when they called my basketball shoes cheap, which they were. A bright sunny day in my memory, I was standing under an awning at our school, wearing my Dikembe Mutombo basketball shoes (black-on-black; $39.99) while everyone else wore their Jordans. A bright, sunny day, but the other kids stood around me in a circle and called my parents cheap and my shoes cheap. They turned their mouths toward the sky in laughter. I ran, bursting through the circle and away. I didn't understand. My parents were poor, but so were everybody else's. Chad was there with them, open mouth turned toward the bright sky. That day even my best friend wouldn't sit with me at lunch.

Another scene, another sunny day. (Do I only remember the rare sunny days, Washington State? Am I imposing the sun onto memories of rainy days?) I was alone at recess and sitting on top of the monkey bars, which we weren't allowed to do. I was silent and still, invisible enough—outside enough—to go unnoticed in my rule breaking. It felt good up there in the sun. I remember thinking, "Chad R. is your last link to cool." Which meant, let him use you. Which meant, don't let go. Cling desperately to him. He has something you don't, your brain and his cool are a fair exchange.

But I didn't. The next week I told him on the phone that I wouldn't help him anymore with his homework unless he wanted to be *real* friends. Translation: Let me come inside. Give me some of your ease and grace and charm. Or at least don't laugh at me with the others.

We all know what his answer was. Chad wasn't about to let me in, and so I stayed outside, but principled. I remained this way for a long, long time.

# 2

I've called him different things. Kaliq in my writing. Tariq on Grindr, setting up our threesomes (or trying to). I got that name from him. For his hookups, he called himself Tariq, one of his middle names, so that his boys couldn't Google him after. They always texted him though, or tried to find him again on Grindr. I've never written down his real name. I know how badly he wants to have people, the world outside, and even his lovers, view him as perfect. And on these pages he won't be—but then again, neither will I.

# 3

When we were together, I couldn't imagine leaving him. He was everything to me, a million things that I couldn't turn away from. He was the type of man I never imagined myself with: beautiful, charming, easy, tall, stylish. Here's what I always had imagined as my man or woman: bookish, awkward, kind. He taught me that being beautiful is also a burden. His beauty preceded him in every interaction he would have, and we all wanted to consume it (and therefore him). Most of his boys didn't want to see him as anything but. I always saw him as more than that, which is why he loved me, and why he kept me outside. I was everything he had waited for. I was dangerous. I was his salvation—how terrifying. His beauty left me chasing him; it left me always outside knocking on a door that only occasionally opened. A door he alone controlled. What freedom to have no control, to simply wait. Yes, the times he let me inside were ecstatic, but mostly I was outside, as I had always been.

# 4

I did things I shouldn't have done. I texted ex-boyfriends. He went through my phone. I messaged boys on FB. He searched my computer. He always found my transgressions, and they kept him on the outside, where he wanted to be. Validated in his hiding. His outside equated vulnerability with weakness. I never saw him cry. He was outside, not letting me in, to keep himself safe. Each of us alone and outside, holding each other at night, for years.

# 5

It was my fault. I asked the question. He said once that if we broke up, the thing he would miss most about me was the food that I cooked for him. Not my body; not my conversation; not how we would laugh together late at night when we were both so tired and wanted to sleep but joked and joked and joked. He would miss my squash most. Pan-roasted butternut squash with maple syrup—the good kind, the expensive kind—and dried chipotle pepper. The key is to let it burn, to let the sugar burn, or caramelize, a crust on the outside that looks ruined but that tastes both sweet and bitter. His roommates laughed at us—at me—because he made me make it every time I cooked. He would offer to take care of dinner, but then beg me to cook the squash. It took almost an hour, but I relented. We ate that squash once a week, at least, for two years. I haven't made it since. I wonder if it's true, if that's what he misses most. I wonder, but I don't know how to ask.

# 6

*Instinctively you give to me*

*The love that I need*

*I cherish the moments with you*

*Respectfully I say to thee*

*I'm aware that you're cheatin'*

*When no one makes me feel like you do*


*Upside down*

*Boy, you turn me*

*Inside out*

*And round and round*


*Upside down*

*Boy, you turn me*

*Inside out*

*And round and round* [1]

---

1   "Upside Down" (1980) by Diana Ross (written by Nile Rodgers and Bernard Edwards).

# 7

He dumped me because one of my friends was rude to him at an event. I changed his name in my phone to Tariq to remind myself that I was nothing more than one of his tricks. As a friend of mine put it, I was just one of the boys he was sleeping with. But that was true even when we were together. Sometimes, when I imagined that we might get back together, when I wanted to think him more than the sex that he still occasionally gave to me, I changed his name in my phone to Kaliq. To remind myself that he was a fiction I had written. And that I could erase.

# 8

I left him once. On our fifth date, the first night I was to stay over, we got drunk together. A bunch of people were over at his apartment. Artists, entertainers—New York's gay inside. I felt included in this world maybe for the first time. Drunk already, I looked down at his phone (on the couch next to him) and it was open to Grindr. Later that night he invited over a mutual friend that I had found frivolous. They all did a line of coke together. I sat and watched. Is this what the inside looks like? I ran away that night, biking home at 4 AM without an explanation. Outside but principled. But I came back to him two weeks later. He missed me. I came back that first time. It was the only time I truly left. After that, I would run away, but never fail to return. There was a force that kept pulling me back to him. A gravity. He was my earth. He was many times my mass. I couldn't escape, not him. Not until the end, when I really was so gone that no email or phone call or late night fucking could bring me back, even when we both tried.

# 9

*That was also the day—*
     *Anne Carson would write of her anti-hero Geryon—*
*That was also the day*
*He began his autobiography.*
*In this work Geryon set down all inside things*
*particularly his own heroism*
*and early death much to the despair of the community.*
*He coolly omitted*
*all outside things.*[2]


This is my autobiography, or one of them, full of things both inside and out. If I have a central fault, it's that my interior walls are too porous—I let too many things, too many people, inside.

2   *Autobiography of Red,* Anne Carson

# 10

I wouldn't let him fuck me raw again after I found out that he had cheated. He wanted us both to get on Truvada so that he could fuck me without a condom, since I couldn't trust him not to lie, to cheat. I swallowed that massive blue pill for a week, and he did for a month, but then we fought and ended up not fucking at all. And by that point I was tired of being pressured to get fucked raw. And at that point, he was tired of my moralizing and talking all the time. At that point, no pill could bring us back.

# 11

He had grace. What is grace if not control over our bodies? I never had that, but he had learned it in movement, in conversation, in sex. So, he taught me how to douche. I had never cared enough before to find what worked for my body. I had used a brand that made me clean but wet. Too wet. He liked a clean bottom every time. So I learned, and his brand worked the best for me too.

I would bike to his place—I was too poor to take the train—douche, shower, and then I would be ready.

But then he started to complain: Why couldn't I come over ready?

We were standing in the hallway between his bedroom and the bathroom he shared with his two roommates, who were also pretty gay boys.

*Because I have to bike, babe, and I get sweaty, and I need to get ready, and it's just easiest if I do it here.* What I meant: I'm not graceful, my body melts and sweats and, if you want me clean, and I know you want me clean, then I need some time. What I meant: I'm your boyfriend and you love me and I love you and that means you don't just get to fuck me, you don't just get that version of my body, you get the before and after, and I don't understand (and I never will understand, not really) why that isn't the best part of this, of this thing we're doing.

What he said: *Fine*.

He didn't like to see the process. He was used to hookups by then: boys who show up ready, fuck, then leave. He liked them showing up ready. And he liked them leaving.

That's fine, babe, but *I'm your boyfriend*, and I have a body, and it sweats, I sweat, when I bike, and I don't have much grace, but I'm learning, and *just give me 20 minutes and then* my body, my body and *I will be* ready (for yours), *ok?*

*Ok babe?*

*Fine.*

# 12

Kaliq is black and from a middle class family. I'm from a poor
white family. We are both men who fuck men. The traumas that we
brought into our love, the traumas that we enacted on one another,
have everything to do with who he is and where he comes from,
who I am and where I come from. You can't take it out of the story
just as you can't take it out of our skin, our bodies, our families,
our memories, our love.

I was trying to love him and to save him, and I imagined these
two things to be one project. I hate how missionary that sounds.
We both needed saving. I'd always viewed caring for others as the
only way to save myself from loneliness. I'd always longed to be a
martyr, as a good Irish Catholic boy might do.

He was trying to love me, I think, without killing himself. Without
erasing himself. He was doing the best he could. I do believe that,
even now. He carried so, so much. He carried things I can't say
here because I still believe in protecting him. So much belongs to
him and not to me, and that includes his blackness. My whiteness
was something he had to survive, too. And when I left, another
trauma for us both to carry. My whiteness was always a thing
between us, and so was the fact that he only fucked white boys,
and so was the fact that my whole life was full of people of color

I loved, some of whom I'd loved by fucking, just as I'd loved him. Our lives were always messy. I didn't mind the mess, I figured it comes with honesty. I had to stop myself from laughing at writing that word—honesty—because we were never quite that with each other, but about somethings we were. About our mess, our hurt, our trauma, his black and mine white and both of ours something like queer, our mess we never hid or told a lie about because we couldn't take it out of our skin, our bodies, our families—and we were sometimes family to each other—our memories, our love, and I do think I would call it love. Even now.

# 13

I always used to wonder: Why do people stay? If you're being abused, why don't you leave? No one is placing a gun to your head, except when they are. I didn't see how two people's insecurities can meet and amplify and grow until they can't walk away. Each person knows they need to, but they can't watch the other person walk away either.

We had survived so much.

I don't wonder why people stay anymore. I didn't stay, not anymore, but I could have, and sometimes I wish I had, and I don't need to wonder because I know how good it can feel when it feels good, how your life can become a chasing of that good feeling, and anyway, I know what that feels like and it doesn't feel all-the-way bad.

# 14

## [REDACTED]3

---

3    Image of an Adam4Adam profile with his picture. One of many such images of profiles he promised he didn't have—not any more—over the years we were together. For legal, practical, ethical reasons, these images have been removed from the text, but their omission is a part of this story. When this story was my own life, the word gaslighting did not yet exist for me. Kaliq lied so much, and so often, about sometimes such trivial things, that I needed, when I sat down and wrote, to have receipts. To document what happened, so—first—I could believe that it had happened, and then so that I could convince you. I always doubt myself, and my own pain is no exception. He'd certainly tell this story differently, but this image, and the ones that follow, are facts; they happened, and they happened to me.

# 15

Writing this will break us forever, though we haven't seen each other in months. Without him, am I inside or out? Writing this will end it. What will I be then? When he reads this, I know what he's going to do. He'll fuck. He'll be hurt, and he won't like how ugly he looks, and he will feel ugly and guilty. He will see my hurt. And he'll fuck. He'll fuck to be wanted. To be craved. The boy, some random boy from Grindr or Facebook or someplace else, will come over ready. Clean. To feel nothing but good. To laugh. To cum. To be able to kick the boy out after. To hurt me. To hurt himself. Just like when we were together.

# 16

I don't want my mother to read this. I know she will.

# 17

His height made him seem consequential. His shaved-short head, too. His chest hair, too. He made me feel small and feminine, like he would take care of me, and, in some ways, I suppose he did.

# 18

When he was upset, or upset with me, he would go out to the gay club. When he was upset with me, he would cheat. I found out on Grindr by messaging a boy whom I knew would be his type. A French boy, of course. The boy was, in fact, his type, so much so that they had been fucking when he and I were supposed to be monogamous.

He did like going out, but never admitted it to me because he didn't want me to see. No, I just wanted to be included, I just wanted to come along. He rarely let me. He rarely let me in to that version of himself. I wouldn't find out about his late nights until later. When we were boyfriends and spent a weekend night apart, I would look for him on Grindr or Adam. I often found him, and had to wait until the morning to confront him about it. Fitful sleep. Whenever a new gay party promoter would post photos on Facebook, I would click through them all wondering when I would find him. I never did, not there.

I wasn't judging his desire for these parties, even if he felt otherwise. I wasn't judging his desire for other boys. I wasn't judging; I just wanted to be there too. Inside.

# 19

You'll call me self-indulgent for writing about my pain, my self. My breakup (again). How many brokenhearted essays does this world already have, and how many more does it need?

I read an interview with an editor where he said never to write about your breakup. What could you possibly add to that conversation by now, he said. Well, I don't know, but I know this: I have to write about this, and I haven't yet read much about how two boys can love and hate and abuse each other. Kiss deep while all the while kicking each other in the shins, and that's what we felt like most days. How we can model our love on the worst of the straight world, beat the shit out of each other just like them, and not know how to walk away, or stop. I haven't seen enough written about that between two boys, so here it is.

# 20

He was the type of boy you can't imagine shitting ever, the type of boy who would never, ever shit on your sheets. Maybe that's why he never, ever let me fuck him. He needed to stay in control.

I shit on his sheets. Once when he was fucking me from behind on the floor. I couldn't smell it, but he could. He stopped. Other times I could smell it, too, but I never was the one who stopped. The worst: once when he was eating me out. *Sorry, babe. Sorry.*

# 21

[REDACTED]⁴

---

4  Picture of the view from inside his window, looking out, winter, from his bed. It's a picture I took from inside his home, inside his room, my favorite place—then—in the world.

# 22

After I split from him for good, he tried to come back. He never could stay gone. He told me all the things he knew I wanted to hear. He said he would do anything to get me back. We would travel together. I would see his hometown, meet his mom. He would come uptown more to see me. He would stop going to his gym, David Barton, which was basically a sex club and where he hooked up in the steam room during our relationship over and over and over. He would join Crunch, a gym that didn't even have steam rooms, which I had asked him to do years earlier. He said no then. He would be better, he wanted to give me the boyfriend I deserved, he said, he wanted to be that man.

When I brought up the past and my inability to believe that this change would mean something when all the others, all the supposed changes before, had not, he said that I was living in the past. Why not just try, babe? Just try it, and let go of the hurt, that's in the past.

# 23

*What I do know is that love reckons with the past and evil reminds us to look to the future. Evil loves tomorrow because peddling in possibility is what abusers do. At my worst, I know that I've wanted the people that I've hurt to look forward, imagining all that I can be and forgetting the contours of who I have been to them.*[5]

---

5    Kiese Laymon on race, abuse, forgiveness. http://www.theguardian.com/commentisfree/2015/jun/23/black-churchesforgive-white-people-shame

# 24

I have come to believe that the things we shame others for doing are things that we desire for ourselves but fear. For example: Truvada raw bottoms; Grindr girls; sex party participants; polyamorous partners. Going back to Freud, isn't the purpose of a taboo to restrict our desires, and why would we need restrictions if we didn't have the desires to begin with? Freud was worried about our mothers, about incest, but then sodomy is also taboo, and maybe something Freud knew a little something about too. But then female sexuality is also taboo, but then group sex is also taboo, but then polyamory is also taboo, but then what Tariq and I did was also taboo. I wanted it then, and much of it I want still. If I'm not actualizing my desires—desires I can't even admit to, really—and other people are, it's easier to shame them than to interrogate my own self. I had always wanted the type of sex we had, but I judged him for it—because I judged myself.

# 25

He taught me to moisturize my face so that I would always stay young, or as much as possible.

# 26

## [REDACTED][6]

---

6    Google Image Search for "Inside Out", mostly stills from the cartoon movie about different feelings at war for the control of a little girl's mind, and thus her mood, and thus her actions.

# 27

One reason I didn't leave him: I was afraid that I would stop writing. I started writing seriously with him, and he always gave me enough confusion and heartache to work out on the page. Or at least he always gave me the courage to put my stuff out there. Somehow I felt that with him as my boyfriend, I could stomach the rejection of the writer's life. No matter what happened, I'd have a hot boyfriend. Always. And, I wrote about him because I could never quite work him out. See, I'm writing about him still because he was a mirror to me, and I never could quite work myself out. See, he showed me the best and worst of myself.

Or he was a muse. And what is a muse but an unrequited love? As he was disappearing from my life, I still cared about words and I still wanted them on the page—which is to say that I still wrote. I realized that a muse is not singular, and life is full of unrequited loves, but none of them should have to break your heart again and again, and if that is what is required to make art then fuck it, I'll just go live.

# 28

We do everything but teach ourselves and one another how to have healthy relationships: vulnerability as weakness; commitment as feminine; sex as a drug. Yes, men may be particularly socialized into unhealthy ways of loving and fucking. Don't believe me? Ask bell. Or your mother. Or mine.

We do everything but teach ourselves and one another how to have healthy relationships, then we pathologize abuse and abusers.

We say not to talk about it. Whispered words. How could s/he? And how could you stay? And really, you shouldn't talk about it much, and not in polite company.

No. I want to see your scars. And here are mine. And here, too, are his.

# 29

In college, my favorite professor did a demonstration that stayed with me all these years. Animal physiology, and we were talking about how things get into and out of the body.

Nothing gets inside the body unless it passes the cells of our epithelium, our inside/out. Our skin can be a barrier, passed. But even our digestive system has its skin: Just because we've swallowed something doesn't mean it's inside of us. It isn't. Not until we let it cross our membrane.

So, the professor said, imagine this. Imagine I swallow a pebble tied to a string. He made the motion, eating the pebble, holding the string. And I wait, he said, for the pebble to pass, but I keep feeding more string. Once the pebble passes, I can floss myself, he said, from mouth to ass, but the entire length of string is outside of my body. It isn't inside, it didn't make it past my cells, my epithelium, my inside/out. It's all up in my gut, he didn't say, but outside my body.

When gay men have sex, we say, sometimes, I want you inside me. The bottom, the one about to get fucked, sometimes has to beg—I need you, he might say, inside me. Sometimes Tariq made me beg, and I loved it.

You could floss yourself with my ex, Tariq, and he'd never be inside. That's how he was: all up in my gut but outside my body. And my insides were coming out.

# 30

*I am a homosexual and a writer, both of whom are professionally self-regarding and self-esteeming creatures.*[7]

---

7    Wayne Koestenbaum quoting Susan Sontag.

# 31

When we were cracking up I did some terrible things. I was lonely and I did what (some) lonely people do. I found other lonely people and tried to make a go of it. It just felt nice to be with someone. I would orbit away from him, from my Kaliq, but the rubber band never snapped. I dreamed of another man providing the energy required to break my orbit, snap the band. It never happened, Kaliq always pulled me back in.

iMessage: Come over.

That's all it took. I ran to him still while telling the boys whom I dated that I was heart broken, and so I broke their hearts. They told me as much. Heartbreak, if not abuse, is self-perpetuating. I knew that in theory but I never thought it would be by me.

# 32

Here are the boys I dated while I dated him. Most of them were after he broke up with me, but was still in my life, and I was so used to being outside. The writer. The fashion student. The doctor. The professor. I'm not ready to tell their stories. They can write them. They can make me look ugly. I fucked up. I'm sorry.

# 33

I realize now, not in writing this but in editing, that "He hurt me" is
not an excuse to hurt others. I fucked up. Forgive me.

# 34

I was sitting on an airplane and writing as if he had given me HIV, and I started to cry. He was cheating with the French boy and others while we were together, yet I trusted him to be raw. I told myself I was crying about disease and fear. But no, no. That wasn't true. What was worse than the fear of HIV was another fear: losing him. HIV could be lived with. I was crying because I was writing about HIV, and I knew that I had to write about HIV, and I was writing about him, and I knew I had to write about him, and I knew that if I wrote about him and HIV and us and how he had hurt me, I knew he would leave and never come back.

I made myself write to make him leave, and I was crying because him leaving was worse than me having any disease. And then he didn't leave. In fact, after those words went out into the world— after I said that he maybe gave me HIV and maybe not—he tried to come back. He tried to come back. My attempt to get away didn't work, but the very fact that I attempted at all began my quest toward something like freedom. What terrible words (quest / freedom); how generic. And here I am doing it again: writing this so that he will stay gone, stay hating me. This is also generic, but true: It started there, at 30,000 feet, between LA and NYC, crying about something but pretending it was about something else.

# 35

See how much I cry? My insides, salty, dripping out and down my cheek. See? But it wasn't a show; I did it when he wasn't even there, when the passengers in seats 26A and 26B were my only audience.

# 36

*In a healthy relationship, both partners respect and trust one another and embrace each other's differences. Both partners are able to communicate effectively their needs and listen to their partner, and work to resolve conflict in a rational and non-violent way. But maintaining a healthy relationship requires skills many young people are never taught. A lack of these skills, and growing up in a society that sometimes celebrates violence or in a community that experiences high rates of violence, can lead to unhealthy and even violent relationships among youth.[8]*

---

8  From http://www.advocatesforyouth.org/datingviolence

# 37

## [REDACTED][9]

---

9  Screen capture of a text message from Tariq :

[ picture of a boy ]

Tonight I want this. He's easy he's sweet he's upfront and not manipulative and until I
meets guys who's the opposite of you and not those things this will do just fine

# 38

He never wanted me to take care of him when he was sick. He never liked to share his body with me when it wasn't under his control. I had to beg to be able to come down, to cook him soup, to just sit next to him on the couch, to touch him just at the ankle, with my ankle. And of course his body was never under his own control. It was falling apart, which is the only thing that bodies ever do. He limped on a bad ankle for the last months he was in my life, but only limped in front of me and not on the street. I knew it still hurt because he wouldn't put weight on it as he stood to clean his room.

Or this: Early on, he had an upset stomach. Bad takeout. I came downtown. He said no, but I came anyway, and then he said thank you. At one point he felt sick to his stomach, and it came on in a rush, and he ran to the bathroom with his hand over his mouth. He didn't make it. His insides came out. And he had let me see it. I felt that this moment would transform us; I felt that he had finally opened up, that he had finally let me see inside. But the door would only ever open like that, in a flash and accidentally, and it would close just as quickly.

This is when I loved him the most, when his insides were coming out and, instead of hiding, he finally let me see.

# 39

## [REDACTED][10]

---

10      Screen capture of a text message from F———:

You good sir?
Yes Joe. Are you?
Miss you. Just saying hi. About to grab dinner and
read some work. Been writing and pitching from lab.
Cool.
Lol. Ok fine. I'll leave you alone.

# 40

Why am I talking so much about sex when I want to be talking about cliques, power, culture, and access? I was a virgin until I was 22, and then I had a monogamous sex life—adventurous always, but only with one person at a time.

I always thought I was smart. I always thought I was kind. I never thought I was beautiful. I never considered myself worthy of a certain type of embodied pleasure.

I never imagined I could even be a slut. Who would want to fuck me, anyway, unless they loved me? That type of sex was something other people got to do (models, celebrities).

He showed me how to do that, and it felt good not because sex feels good, which it usually does, but because I finally was the type of boy who could get laid on Grindr, and he showed me how.

# 41

*But I am not yet sure how to sever the love from the lover without occasioning some degree of carnage,* Maggie Nelson wrote in *Bluets.*

"It is time for carnage," I responded in the margin years ago, but after Kaliq and I broke. Seeing my response to Maggie's words, reading them today, I cried. Carnage, it would turn out, was necessary. Carnage, it would turn out, hurts like hell.

# 42

Even, and maybe especially, a Friday night at his house felt special because he was there. Week after week, we sat on the couch and watched bad movies and ate food that he or I cooked and cuddled on the couch. I was just one of the boys he was sleeping with. I was the one he chose to share that night with, if only that night, and it was a gift, because he was there, giving it to me.

# 43

[REDACTED][11]

---

11  Selfies (from left to right):

1.    Selfie with my face covered by the phone in the gay bar across the street from his house, a bar I went to before I knew Kaliq, a bar I go to still.
2.    Selfie naked in a bathroom mirror, my hands covering my dick, my balls, the phone covering my face.
3.    Selfie naked in the same bathroom mirror, my entire body exposed, the phone covering my face.
4.    Selfie in the window of a New York City subway train, maybe an A train, uptown. The phone covers my face.

Look at my body. He taught me how to do this, or some of it.

# 44

Kaliq is a character in a book that I wrote that no one wants to publish. I called our story non-fiction, but the book is a novel because it contains three other stories, made up. It takes place during a disaster, natural: Hurricane Sandy. Editors, agents, publishers, when they wrote back, told me that the narrative is too fragmented, that readers will fail to enter fully into any one story because of the way the perspective continues to change over and over and over. How else could I manage to write about him? I failed to enter the story fully myself, and even so I barely managed to survive.

# 45

## MAPLE/CHIPOTLE BUTTERNUT SQUASH

Cut a whole butternut squash into roughly one-inch squares (the larger, the longer they will take to cook). Grind one half of a dried chipotle pepper with a mortar and pestle. Get a large skillet very hot and add the squash. Salt liberally with kosher salt and add the crushed dried chipotle. If you desire more spice (the chipotle is smoky and mild) add crushed red pepper or cayenne pepper. Let the squash brown; add half a cup high-quality maple syrup and caramelize squash until it is quite brown. Black even. Let it burn. It really must caramelize, grow a crust on the outside that looks ruined but that tastes both sweet and bitter. Add olive oil (2 tablespoons) and reduce heat to medium; simmer until the squash is cooked through, roughly 45 minutes. Finish with a touch more maple syrup if you have a sweet tooth—he did—and coarse ground pink Hawaiian sea salt.

# 46

## [REDACTED]¹²

---

12      Grindr chat with a French boy who was fucked by Tariq when we were together and
supposedly monogamous.

[ Selfie]

[ Picture of Tariq ]

I know your man already.

Tell him the French boy.

When did you see him last?

You're hot dude.

Interested in us together?

It's been a while.

March probably.

But yes.

# 47

Would I be Diego or Frida? What if I told you that he was an artist too?

# 48

Paris was the beginning of our relationship, and the end. The email that brought me back to him after the first time—the only time—I left told me about a night in Paris. He was out clubbing with fashion kids, late dinners with minor celebrities or their stylists, and he came home and just wanted to be with me. We had only met once, but for whatever reason I came to mind.

Paris broke us when he left me for it. I helped him put together his application for a fellowship that would land him there for a month, but when he got it he told me he would be working, and he didn't want me to come. No, he said it stronger: I was not allowed to come. But he wanted to be open. He wanted to go off to Paris to work with artists and designers and dancers and DJs, to film nightlife, and I couldn't come, and he wanted to have sex, and I wasn't invited, and that's just how it always was, that's just how it always had been, and how I knew it would be, from my childhood until now. I was outside.

It broke me from him.

Only I didn't realize it because I was too afraid to lose him. I was too afraid to not even have a door to knock on. I was too afraid to not even have someone to aspire to, someone who might, someday, have the ability to let me in.

# 49

Kaliq loved that I spoke and read French. He loved Paris, and French boys. He loved me for a time. He wanted to learn French, too. He believed that after a few months, once a week, he'd be fluent, like me. I never called myself fluent anyway; and a month or three isn't enough, no matter how many times a week. I always loved him for his enthusiasm, though, his boyish ability to go into something believing it would work out for the best, and quickly. It was a life skill I didn't have. After a few months, frustrated at how little he'd learned, he quit taking classes, but still got so excited to tell all his friends, everyone we met, about how I spoke this language he so adored. That he adored it as much for the boys he'd been with before—and during—our relationships always went unstated, but understood, at least by me.

# 50

*Je n'ai jamais écrit, croyant le faire, je n'ai jamais aimé, croyant aimer, je n'ai jamais rien fait qu'attendre devant la porte fermée.*[13]

*(I've never written and believed that I was writing, I've never loved, believing I was loving, I've never done anything except wait outside a closed door.)*

---

13 *The Lover*, Marguerite Duras

# 51

He told me that he didn't want to bottom for me ever again because I liked it too much. Watching me get off to him fucking me— watching me love it so much, beg for it sometimes—made him see me that way and only that way. Thirsty bottom, he would whisper in my ear as he fucked me. It always made me hard. Especially later, after he watched other boys fuck me too. The first time a boy fucked me in front of Kaliq they both came quickly, at the same time, on my back. I was on all fours. I was nowhere near done. The boy got up and left, and Kaliq played with my nipples until I came sitting on his couch. I wanted to hold him—what an experience we had just had together. He asked for it, set it up, picked the boy, set the time. I just showed up. But no, he was cold, distant, obviously upset but unwilling to admit it. I tried to sit next to him on the couch and he kept moving away.

It took days for him to see or hug me again. We texted, and he would take hours to reply. He couldn't see me, this boy who took his dick and sometimes others, as someone whom he also loved and cared for. But he loved seeing me like that too; he needed it. He always said he needed to dirty me up, sexually. After he told me that he didn't care much for our sex. He needed both, and knew they couldn't both exist in one person, not for him. After all that he couldn't see me as someone aggressive, which is what he needed in a top. I had lost that energy—he would call it "that vibe"—and I never got it back. In our last year together, I never fucked him at all. Not once. He promised that in all of his cheating (what was it babe, 30 boys?), no one else did either. But I don't believe it.

# 52

He talked about our partnership in terms of battle, strategy, and punishment. A war embodied. If I was upset about something, he thought that I was putting him on punishment and would say so. No, I would always say, I'm just telling you how I feel. I have emotions, and here they are. If he was upset, he punished me by disappearing—or worse, by cheating—but he would only admit to that later, much later. If I was upset, I would cry. That simple. Inside/out.

# 53

By the way, he never hit me, not once. That's not what I mean by abuse. Actually, I'm the one who hit him. We got drunk and went out to a bar in NYC notorious for low-level public sex, naked dancers. The Cock. I loved seeing him in that bar, sharing it. That night, he liked one of the dancers, kept touching him. On the walk home, I told him to get on Grindr, find a third if he wanted. So he did. We got home, and no thirds were coming (except a boy who wanted us raw), so I got naked and showered and made sure my insides were clean for him, and then I waited for him in bed. And waited. And waited.

He was on Grindr in the living room, and I was waiting, naked, to have sex with him in his own bed. This wasn't the first time this happened.

I had to text him to get him to come back to his room, and even then it took a while. I was pissed, and we fought a little bit, and then I wanted to fuck, still, because that's what I had wanted all night: him. He rolled over and feigned sleep after all that. I flipped out, and he ignored me. I kicked the bed. I punched his shoulder.

I punched his shoulder. Then he flipped out, got in my face, went to the couch, came back to bed. Then we slept. I think I liked not being wanted sometimes. How fucked up is that. That he always wanted others more, I liked that. And abuse, if that's what this was, and I think it was, is a reflexive verb. I punched his shoulder because it was the only thing that I could do to be heard, and that was me taking my control, and it was ugly. How could I do such a thing? How?

# 54

I realize now that the fact that the sex was good doesn't matter much. The point is that I was kept outside, even of the sex, our sex, by him or by myself, and it doesn't matter which.

# 55

Years later, I got my first tattoo, a capital letter F on my bicep and ass, after the Paul Monette poem ranting against William F. Buckley's notion of a tattoo for HIV positive people. Two tattoos really, to mark two sites on the body, but tattoos—Buckley was not a monster after all—that could be hidden by clothing on the street. Monette was a fag, his word, and HIV positive. He died of the virus before effective treatments were developed.

*I want my F for fag of course on the left / bicep twined with a Navy anchor deck / of Luckies curled in my tee sleeve just the look / to sport through a minefield beating a path / to smithereens arm in arm friend & friend*

I got the tattoo to mark my body as desirable using the very word that had—for years—been used to bully it. Only after my friend began digging ink permanently into my skin did I realize that the capital letter F might also stand for, symbolize, his real first name, that name I've never written down, F———.

My tattoo artist—a close friend—talked about boundaries used by some other artists: Don't tattoo someone when they're drunk; Don't tattoo couples, they're bound to break up.

*I wouldn't mind*, I said, *having a tattoo of an ex's name on my skin. I carry all of them, every one of them, in my body, anyway, and the pain of that feels visible even though it isn't. Even him*, and I said his name and realized that his name, a part of it, was even then being sliced into my skin pixel by pixel.

The next day, the F on my arm kept surprising me, and yes it did make me think of him, but it made me think of my own name first, what I call myself, what I love now. I am a faggot. He couldn't show me that. I had to teach myself.

# 56

But I started to get off to it though, too, didn't I babe? We both did. He would tell me the details of the times he cheated, and I learned to love it. I jerked off to it. The hottest though was this: He would tell me that I would never be enough for him, not ever, and I believed him and knew it to be true. He would put his fingers inside, pull them back out, as though it were the most boring thing he'd been obligated to do that day, and I would cum—my insides coming out—shooting all over my chest, harder than I ever had.

# 57

*I reminded her that my whole upbringing had been devoted to preventing me from becoming a slut; I then gave a brief description of my personal life, offering each detail as evidence that my upbringing had been a failure and that, in fact, life as a slut was quite enjoyable, thank you very much.*[14]

He taught me that, or some of it.

---

14    From *Lucy: A Novel* by Jamaica Kincaid

# 58

It's easier to miss someone when they stay gone. I wished he had moved to Portland for that job. I considered a job in Minnesota but didn't get it. Even when we were still together or sleeping together, I just wanted anything to carry him away from me or me away from him. To save myself. To save him.

# 59

If Paris was the end, and I knew it would be, it looked like this.

Like a whimper. We had plans for his last night in NYC. I was planning—of course—to cook him dinner. Squash. What else?

To say goodbye.

But he fucked up the day. Of course. And so I got a call at work.

*Oh my flight is tonight.*

*What? Tonight?*

*Sorry—so?*

*I'll come by your work... to say goodbye.*

*Ok. Ok fine.*

He ended up missing his flight anyway, but not rebooking for the next day to come home and fuck and cook and eat and laugh. No, he flew out that night, four hours later. So that's how we said goodbye.

# 60

He didn't stay gone. He tried to come back. It was, of course, almost the exact day that I gave up on him. When I decided I didn't care who he was fucking, what he was doing, whether or not he texted. After two years of caring about those things more than almost anything else, it was a freedom I wasn't expecting. I had gotten used to constant worry, and I only recognized it when it was gone. My chest had felt tight for a year—more. I only realized when I was free of it. That's when he tried to come back, and when I said no. Six months after he got home from Paris. Oh, he said everything he knew I had been waiting years to hear, but the words didn't sound the same, and anyway, I wasn't waiting for that, not anymore.

# 61

One of our first threesomes, from Grindr of course, ended up being an artist, and so of course that boy was over at Tariq's house for a house party one weekend I was out of town. He only ever had house parties when he knew I couldn't come. A year later, Kaliq interviewed this boy for his website. Or I suppose we did, together. He often let me (had me? made me?) write interview questions for artists. I wrote the questions and emailed them to Kaliq, who reformatted them and emailed them to the boy, who answered as though they were chatting face-to-face, full of banter. Kaliq formatted the questions and posted the piece online. See this is me, not him: IN THE WORLD WHERE THE GAY AGENDA SEEMS TO BE FOCUSED ON ASSIMILATION INTO STRAIGHT INSTITUTIONS (THE MILITARY, MARRIAGE), HAS THERE BEEN ANY PUSHBACK FROM THE GAY COMMUNITY ABOUT THE SEXUAL NATURE OF YOUR WORK?

My name is nowhere on the published interview.

I wonder how I would answer my own question now.

# 62

Years later, after all this, Facebook would suggest an event to me. Apparently, enough of my friends were interested or going that it popped up on my timeline. Clicking over, I found one of those Brooklyn warehouse parties—a Halloween, backroom, anything-goes party. Yes, we have those on Facebook now. Not a sex party really, but a club party with sex. It was hosted by this artist, the one we met through our threesome, the one we interviewed together. I'm sure he doesn't remember my name. On the list of hosts, there he was: F———. His own name, not hidden, not a behind-the-scenes DJ, not a pseudonym, but his name. F———, and not Tariq. You could Google him if you wanted. And years later, all of this came back. All this.

All of this came back. Part of me, my better part, was proud of him. Happy for him. Proud that he was owning his desires, his needs, that he was willing to name them so publicly when he had hid them from me, who always stood outside, for years. Part of me, years later, was gutted, outside and not invited, not acknowledged or invited to this party, one I didn't want to go to anyway, but one that I wanted to go to. I wasn't anyone to him, not anymore. There it was, his own name on the poster, and I didn't go, not even just to see him, not even just to stand alone outside.

# 63

He didn't give me HIV.

# 64

There were times when I knew I was being abused. When he said: I'm just not that into our sex. Or: the times he cheated and lied. Or: when he said: You don't understand that you can't just be a wife, you have to be a lover too. The implication (later stated): He wouldn't have cheated if I cut my hair more often, if I wore my contacts more often, which he always said he liked. He liked to see my eyes. I preferred to hide behind my glasses, they made me more comfortable, particularly in social situations. Later, way later, when he was trying to undo the harm, the hurt, the abuse that he would not name as such, he explained his motivations. He never meant to hurt, he just wanted me to show that I cared for him. Or: Sometimes he wanted to hurt, but only because he was hurt and unsafe himself. Later he promised never again baby never ever again, I hear what you're saying and I'm sorry, but by then it was, I decided, just too late.

# 65

*When I write, I'm always* not yet *a poet; I'm a striver, a yearner, hoping to crash the House of Poetry.* **I stand outside,** *like Stella Dallas, hungering. Crane must have felt like an outsider to Poetry. He wrote high because he wanted to* **push his way in.**[15]

Writing is a love I've always imagined myself outside of, too. Writing is a world that I could never quite imagine as my own. I see myself standing at the door of the literary world, and it occasionally opens, and those moments feel transcendent, but I know—because he taught me—that this feels like love and like abuse, both, and that so many queer writers and brown and black writers and trans writers and women writers and disabled writers feel this way no matter how deep they seemingly make it in the literary establishment.

Writing, like being with Kaliq, never quite seemed like a choice. Writing made being with Kaliq, and the boys that came after him, harder. My body, so exposed. The boys have come and gone, but writing has stayed, and on the best of days I see a hatchet in my hands, and in the hands of my friends. On the best of days, we seem poised to break down the door—to turn it from solid wood to kindling, a chore I had growing up with the hatchet my dad gave

---

15  Wayne Koestenbaum on poet Hart Crane. Emphasis mine and his. Emphasis ours.

me when I was (what?) eight or nine—that has so long kept us all on the outside.

# 66

I worry that it isn't really too late, that I might still go back to him and to all this, and so I list the things he did to me and the things I did to him and the list is long. I burn it and start again. Burn. Start again.

# 67

He never liked taking photographs with me. He said he needed his pictures to be taken by a professional photographer so he would look like he had when he modeled. I barely have any photos of us together as proof that his beauty was once mine.

There was a part of me that wishes that he had given me HIV. A physical connection between us. Something from his body that I would carry in mine forever. Proof that he was once mine.

# 68

When we were breaking apart after Paris, that summer I met a boy, another writer, who quickly became a friend. He always wore a cap, and I figured it was his look, a somewhat writerly affectation that actually looked good on him. I told him about the boy that broke me. So he opened up, took off his cap. It turns out he had a boy too, a pretty boy, who broke him. My friend left, but it hurt, and he made bad decisions, painful and reckless decisions, like getting a tattoo on his back and neck and head, a tattoo all over his head. He never finished it, the tattoo; his heartbreak healed enough before he could save up the money or make the time.

We do it to ourselves. The beloved is just a mirror reflecting our own trauma back onto ourselves in ways we find attractive, and thus run toward, when we have become so practiced at running away. I'm running away again, I hope, toward the version of myself that I like more, or at least that I trust more. Principled but outside, again, by choice.

# 69

*I paint myself because I*
*am alone*
*I am the subject I*
*know*
*best[16]*

# 70

He hated how much I cry. My insides coming out. He called it emotionally manipulative. I said it was just my feelings. But no, in his bad moments, my feelings were not my own; they were being used to change how he felt, to change him, to make him feel bad. I always wanted to fight and cry and then commune and come up with solutions and then fuck and sleep. The latter was designed to rebuild a future and to remind us of what was good.

He couldn't fuck after fighting, especially if I had cried.

Lying in his bed, late night, my cheeks wet, eyes red, puffy. *I just can't see you as sexual right now. You were crying 10 minutes ago. Lets just go to sleep. Lets just go to sleep...*

Did I see this as abuse? Should I have? Or was I the abuser for demanding sex so plainly, and for crying harder and harder because I knew it wouldn't come?

# 71

/ you can't make homes out of human beings / someone should
have already told you that /[17]

---

[17]    From Warsan Shire, "for women who are 'difficult' to love."

# 72

I only tried to hurt him twice. Once, he had spent an afternoon texting me at work. We were broken up but still fucking, and he spent the afternoon telling me he was going to have a threesome with two boys in his neighborhood, a threesome with them and not me. He said he didn't give a shit if I didn't want him to do it, he dumped my lame ass, my uptight ass, and he got to do whatever he wanted. This went on for hours. He sent me photos of the two boys, a couple, who lived together and just down the block from him.

I told him two things that I knew would hurt him.

1) That my friends had hated him all along, just like he always worried. This wasn't true. They hadn't, but they had all—by this point—turned against our relationship, and it's not hard to see why.

2) That I was writing about him. About us. About everything.

# 73

See: I can be ugly too. I can be abusive. Did you doubt it?

When I'd written about him before, or he'd seen himself in my work, he went silent or disappeared for a time, either to ease his own pain or because he knew it would hurt me. He hated seeing himself on the page and hated that it was public even more.

I lived that moment knowing it would be a scene on a page. This scene. This page. Maybe I lived that moment to give me something worth committing to a page, a scene dramatic enough to sum up why I loved him, and why I had to leave.

# 74

It's winter, spitting freezing rain. I'm walking, leaving work, it's dark and I walk close to the buildings to be shielded from the weather. I know this will hurt him, and I want it to because he looked ugly that afternoon, and so did I, and while I am apparently happy to share my ugly with the world, it remains his worst nightmare. Into the phone I say, *Kaliq, I'm writing about you.* He couldn't stand to be made ugly, not publicly, not even privately. Ugly was his outside, the only inside I knew.

He tells me he's lying about the threesome; he's going to see a show his friend is in. He was doing it just to fuck with me.

I hang up on him and then don't answer his calls, three of them straight to voice mail. And so, that night, once the freezing rain stops, he goes ahead and has his promised threesome with the two white boys on his block, boyfriends.

He tells me all this later that week when I come over, when I come over because I didn't know how to not, not yet. He tells me about it and it makes me cum, his fingers inside me, coaxing my insides out.

# 75

He told me once, when we were breaking, that he can do bad all by himself. Sex parties, threesomes, boys boys boys. That cuts to the heart of it, doesn't it? As much as he used his power to control me, I knew the end was coming but couldn't let go. I couldn't let go partly because I wanted him and partly because the idea of someone else having him (and his sex) made me crazy. I wanted to control his bad in order to make it my own. That's not love.

I can do bad all on my own. Yes, my love, you can. And so can I. I can do bad; I can do good; I'm sure I'll do both, but on my own, for now, on my own, or at least without you. Outside your world, finally principled.

# 76

After we ended, he made a production of not fucking anyone for 90 days. He was trying to win me back. To show me that he could abstain. That he was more Kaliq than Tariq. No, in fact, that he was nothing but F———. I wanted none of them. By this point, if I wanted anyone, it would have been Tariq. I wanted the sex. But I wanted more than that from life, from a man. When he posted to Instagram, he would hashtag with how many days he had kept his promise, once spoken out loud and to me. #Day49. So I would know. I checked in on him daily.

When he was in Paris, he more or less refused to talk to me. Skyping was a nuisance, and with the time difference and his foreign phone, even texting was rare. But I could tell when he was making love or fucking by the music he would play, posted automatically from Spotify to Facebook. He had songs that were just for fucking. That's how I knew.

When the 90 days were over the hashtags ended. The last one: #Day91. And then his men's fashion week posts started: back to life as normal, Kaliq and Tariq both. Outside my life. Inside my writing still. I believe that everyone I ever loved I will love forever, no matter what. Now I am blocked from his Facebook.

Not even his music, posted automatically from Spotify, can betray those moments when he goes online or when he goes out to find another body or soul to touch, can betray specifically that moment when he lays them down on his bed with its view out the window, back alley, once my own view, but never only mine, to give himself away fully, to let his insides show, if only ever for a moment. I work only blocks from his house, less than a mile from where he still lives, from where he still fucks. From where he gives himself to boys I will never know of. I think about this moment still, looking up at his window, walking outside on the street below.

# INSIDE/OUT

# ACKNOWLEDGMENTS

This project was a hard one to write, and it's harder still to imagine others reading it. I wouldn't have been able to finish this book without the constant and unwavering support of my dearest family of friends. Thank you for helping me survive this time and giving me the courage to write it down as I went. Whitney, Ray, Hala, Jesse, and everyone else: I love you. Greg, you gave me much courage to move forward, to write. Thank you, L. To my family: I'm sorry, and thanks for putting up with this and so much else. I owe so much to my writing workshop, who saw and fixed an early draft of this book—Yana Calou and Ariel Kates and Liz Latty and Ely Shipley and Ricardo Hernandez. Thanks are due to Katie Kotchman who knows when to push and when to coddle and who sees the best in what I do. To Paul Mpagi Sepuya: Thank you for growing up with me as an artist, for placing your body next to my own, for giving this book its perfect cover. To my teachers Kiese Laymon and Randall Kenan and Alex Chee and Darnell Moore, words aren't enough. Finally, to Bryan and Seth at Sibling Rivalry, thank you for seeing something worthwhile in this weird little book, for caring for it with such love and attention, and for birthing it into the world to breathe on its own.

# THE/AUTHOR

Joseph Osmundson is a scientist, writer, and educator from rural Washington State. He has a PhD in Molecular Biophysics from The Rockefeller University and is an Assistant Clinical Professor in Biology at NYU. His writing—about bodies and health, race and identity, sexuality and desire—has appeared in *The Village Voice*, *The Kenyon Review*, *The Los Angeles Review of Books*, *Gawker*, *The Rumpus*, *The Los Angeles Review*, and *The Feminist Wire*, where he is an Associate Editor. His first book, *Capsid: A Love Song* (Indolent Books), won a POZ award for best writing on HIV and was a finalist for a Lambda Literary Award. He's been supported by fellowships from The Lambda Literary Foundation and the New York Foundation for the Arts. He co-hosts the podcast *Food 4 Thot* alongside three friends who share his interest in dick, drama, and discourse, and he can be found tweeting his (sad) feelings all day, everyday.

# THE/PRESS

Sibling Rivalry Press is an independent press based in Little Rock, Arkansas. It is a sponsored project of Fractured Atlas, a nonprofit arts service organization. Contributions to support the operations of Sibling Rivalry Press are tax-deductible to the extent permitted by law, and your donations will directly assist in the publication of work that disturbs and enraptures. To contribute to the publication of more books like this one, please visit our website and click *donate*.

Liz Ahl

Stephanie Anderson

Priscilla Atkins

John Bateman

Sally Bellerose & Cynthia Suopis

Jen Benka

Dustin Brookshire

Sarah Browning

Russ Bunge

Michelle Castleberry

Don Cellini

Philip F. Clark

Risa Denenberg

Alex Gildzen

J. Andrew Goodman

Sara Gregory

Karen Hayes

Wayne B. Johnson & Marcos L. Martínez

Jessica Manack

Alicia Mountain

Rob Jacques

Nahal Suzanne Jamir

Bill La Civita

Mollie Lacy

Anthony Lioi

Catherine Lundoff

Adrian M.

Ed Madden

Open Mouth Reading Series

Red Hen Press

Steven Reigns

Paul Romero

Erik Schuckers

Alana Smoot

Stillhouse Press

KMA Sullivan

Billie Swift

Tony Taylor

Hugh Tipping

Eric Tran

Ursus Americanus Press

Julie Marie Wade

Ray Warman & Dan Kiser

Anonymous (14)

CPSIA information can be obtained
at www.ICGtesting.com
Printed in the USA
LVHW07s1235060518
576193LV00021B/179/P

9 781943 977444